DAVID BECKHAM

DAVID BECKHAM

JASPER RAVENWOOD

CONTENTS

Introduction

David Beckham is one of the most recognizable athletes in the world and a timeless celebrity. His marketability and popularity positioned him at the forefront of sports media during his career, completely redefining the modern-day athlete. Beckham's myriad haircut and style changes made him a point of reference in streetwear style and a prominent figure in print media. Additionally, his impressive record of 781 direct goal contributions in competitions and numerous triumphs established him as one of the best minority football owners today and a qualified football authority, as well as a style couturier. This essay is structured into three comprehensive chapters, each carefully discussing the wide-ranging impact and legacy of David Beckham.

In this essay, I argue that David Beckham formed a composite in global sports, fashion, and music multimedias, intensifying his accessibility and influence in ways that were unprecedented among his predecessors. The former British national captain explicitly embodied 21st-century professionalism and power, solidifying his legend as both a footballer and a fashion icon. It is crucial to recognize what success means for both sports and fashion professionalism. In the following chapters, I will illustrate how Beckham designed much of the off-pitch style for the contemporary athlete by controlling his very own trademarks, such as the iconic marks DAVID BECKHAM, DB7, and DB23, during his active career. First, I will explain how Beckham shifted the entire concept of labor in an era of change and expansion, and then how he updated the notion of sport work to include the elegance of the sport worker.

David Beckham's rise to stardom is a remarkable journey that transcends the boundaries of football, reaching into the realms of fashion, entertainment, and business. His influence stretches far beyond the pitch, where his impeccable sense of style, charisma, and business acumen have made him a global icon. Beckham's story is one of innovation and transformation, showcasing how an athlete can leverage their platform to create a multi-faceted legacy.

Background and Context

The late-20th and early-21st centuries have witnessed groundbreaking evolution in many fields, especially in sports and entertainment. Our newly emerging era of social networking, internet culture, and reality television, with prevalent celebrity lifestyles and ever-expanding economies, brings to mind star athletes such as Cristiano Ronaldo and Lionel Messi. Their performances on the field and the contracts they secured, often exceeding USD 60 million in value, make them extravagant both on and off the pitch.

David Beckham, a retired English attacking midfielder, stands among these soccer legends. Over his 19-year playing career, his natural talent, striking physical characteristics, personality, associations, and corporate interests made him an unprecedented magnetic figure. Although Beckham undoubtedly possesses exceptional soccer skills, the infrastructure surrounding him forged the Beckham brand and his various global enterprises. Beckham played a direct role in transforming the game from a romantic, diverse soccer world into a system of pre-packaged, interchangeable celebrities. His iconic distinctiveness has distributed personality and lifestyle, transforming the way sports fans worldwide perceive soccer. Thus, he is revered not only for the innate talent he brought to the game but also for other, non-sport-related reasons. This exploration delves into Beckham's dual legacy as a footballer and style icon.

In the context of global sports and entertainment, Beckham's career coincided with significant technological advancements and shifts in media consumption. The rise of the internet and social media platforms allowed athletes to connect with fans in unprecedented ways, creating personal brands that could be monetized and leveraged for various business ventures. Beckham was at the forefront of this movement, expertly navigating the evolving landscape to build a powerful and enduring brand.

Beckham's appeal extended beyond his athletic prowess. His relationship with Victoria Adams, a member of the iconic pop group Spice Girls, elevated his celebrity status and introduced him to a broader audience. The couple became a symbol of modern celebrity culture, embodying the intersection of sports, music, and fashion. Their influence was felt across multiple industries, making them one of the most recognizable and influential couples in the world.

In addition to his on-field achievements, Beckham's fashion choices and partnerships with top designers and brands solidified his status as a style icon. His ability to seamlessly transition between different roles—athlete, model, entrepreneur—highlighted his versatility and appeal. Beckham's collaborations with brands such as Adidas, H&M, and his own line of grooming products showcased his keen sense of style and business acumen.

Beckham's impact on the commercialization of soccer cannot be overstated. He played a pivotal role in popularizing the sport in the United States, where soccer was traditionally less prominent. His move to Major League Soccer's LA Galaxy in 2007 was a landmark moment, bringing international attention to the league and inspiring a new generation of soccer fans. Beckham's presence in MLS helped elevate the sport's profile in America, paving the way for future international stars to join the league.

The commercialization of Beckham's image also extended to various philanthropic endeavors. He has been involved in numerous charitable activities, leveraging his fame and resources to support causes such as children's education and health. Beckham's commitment to giving back further enhanced his public image, demonstrating that he was not only a successful athlete and businessman but also a compassionate and socially responsible individual.

Throughout his career, Beckham faced numerous challenges and controversies. From his high-profile transfer from Manchester United to Real Madrid to his stint with LA Galaxy and subsequent loans to AC Milan, his career decisions were often scrutinized by the media and fans. Despite the ups and downs, Beckham's resilience and ability to reinvent himself ensured that he remained relevant and influential.

Beckham's legacy as a footballer is intertwined with his contributions to fashion and entertainment. He was among the first athletes to fully embrace the potential of media and marketing, using his platform to create a multifaceted brand that transcended sports. Beckham's influence on the modern athlete's role is evident in the way today's sports stars manage their public images and engage with their audiences.

In summary, David Beckham's journey from a talented footballer to a global icon is a testament to his vision, determination, and adaptability. He redefined what it means to be an athlete in the 21st century, blending sports, fashion, and business into a cohesive and influential brand. Beckham's dual legacy as a football titan and style maven continues to inspire and shape the worlds of sports and entertainment.

Chapter 1: Beckham's Early Years

David Beckham was born on May 2, 1975, in Leytonstone, East London. As the middle child of three siblings, Beckham inherited his energetic and showy personality from his parents. His father, Ted Beckham, was a kitchen fitter in London's East End and a passionate fan of Manchester United. His mother, Sandra Beckham, was a hairdresser. Like many boys his age, David would watch football matches with his father every Saturday afternoon, sparking a lifelong love for the game.

Beckham's early fascination with football was complemented by his interest in fashion, which set him apart even as a child. In his autobiography, "My Side," Beckham confessed that he was obsessed with fashion and disliked wearing the school uniform or any clothing chosen by teachers. He often wore flamboyant tracksuits that defied the school dress code, highlighting his early flair for style. Football was a significant part of his school life, and Beckham's talent was evident as he played for the school football team. When he moved to a different school closer to home, his passion for football remained strong, leading him to join the new school's team as well as the local county team.

Beckham began his formal football career with the Tottenham Hotspur youth squad. However, his trajectory changed at age 14 when he signed a contract with Manchester United. Sir Alex Ferguson, the legendary manager of Manchester United, was quickly impressed by the young talent and made a pivotal decision to include Beckham in senior team training sessions. This decision, made at the last moment, would change Beckham's life forever. In August 1992, at the age of 17, David Beckham made his debut appearance for Manchester United, hoping to support his family financially. Despite initially struggling to secure a spot on the first team, Beckham's indomitable spirit and hard work earned him acclaim and admiration across the Premiership, attracting interest from top teams such as Liverpool and Real Madrid.

Childhood and Youth Career

David Robert Joseph Beckham was born into a modest family in Essex. His father, Ted, a fervent Manchester United supporter, played a significant role in shaping David's passion for football. They would often attend West Ham United games, which kindled young David's enthusiasm for the sport. Beckham's football talent was soon recognized, and around 1986, he was spotted by a talent scout from Manchester United's Football Academy. The emotional moment when Beckham was invited to join the club marked the beginning of his professional journey.

Beckham spent his formative years at the Manchester United Academy, which became his second home for the next seven years. His early days at the academy were characterized by rigorous training and a deep immersion in football culture. Under the guidance of Sir Alex Ferguson, Beckham's potential was nurtured, and he was allowed to train and travel with the first team at just 17 years of age. Beckham fondly recalls this period as a "fascinating experience," often seeking autographs from club legends like Mark Hughes and Bryan Robson.

Sir Alex Ferguson's support was instrumental in Beckham's development. Recognizing his potential, Ferguson ensured that Beckham balanced his football training with his education, allowing him to train with the first team after school hours. Beckham's dedication to football became evident as he spent countless hours practicing and honing his skills. His introduction to first-team training was a significant milestone, giving him the opportunity to learn from seasoned professionals and experience the intensity of top-tier football.

During his time in the academy, Beckham initially played as a left-sided midfielder, a position that allowed him to develop his versatility and understanding of the game. It wasn't until later in his career that he would become renowned for his role as a right winger, known for his precise crosses and set-piece prowess. Beckham's journey through the ranks of the Manchester United youth system laid the foundation for his future success, shaping him into a player capable of making a significant impact on the world stage.

Beckham's early years were marked by a blend of football and fashion, interests that would later define his public persona. His distinctive style and charisma set him apart from his peers, attracting attention both on and off the pitch. Beckham's ability to balance his football commitments with his passion for fashion and media was a testament to his multifaceted personality and drive to excel in multiple arenas.

As Beckham continued to develop as a player, his reputation grew. His performances for the youth teams earned him a place in the senior squad, and he began to make regular appearances for Manchester United. Beckham's journey from a young, passionate footballer to a global icon was just beginning, and his early experiences in East London and Manchester would shape the trajectory of his remarkable career.

Chapter 2: Beckham's Professional Football Career

David Beckham is well-known for his illustrious career at Manchester United, but his journey in professional football was even more remarkable. Beckham's career spanned from 1993 to 2013, encompassing 20 years of dedication and excellence on the pitch. Throughout this period, Beckham played for several top-tier clubs and made significant contributions to his national team, leaving an indelible mark on the sport.

In the seventeen years of his club career, Beckham displayed immense loyalty and teamwork, both on and off the pitch. His career at Manchester United, in particular, cemented his image as a dedicated and influential figure in football. Beckham's allegiance to Manchester United, symbolized by the iconic number 7 jersey, made him a role model for future generations of footballers. This chapter critically analyzes Beckham's professional career, divided into key periods and relationships within the football world, based on detailed readings of various reports, newspapers, autobiographies, and expert analyses.

Manchester United Years

At the age of 16, as a product of Old Trafford's youth academy, Beckham made his first appearance for Manchester United in 1992. Eventually, he would go on to make 394 appearances for the club, gathering invaluable experiences during his time there. In the summer that Beckham cemented himself as a United regular, the club defied the odds and captured a league and cup double under the leadership of Scottish manager Sir Alex Ferguson. Beckham's influence at the club lasted for 12 years before transferring to Real Madrid, where he scored 85 goals. Throughout his career, Beckham played for several clubs, including Paris Saint-Germain, AC Milan, and a second spell at AC Milan.

During his years at United, Beckham became one of the most well-known footballers globally, leading star-studded lineups alongside the likes of Ryan Giggs, Paul Scholes, and the future "World's Best" wonder kid, Cristiano Ronaldo. This group of players and staff, with Sir Alex Ferguson at the helm, were nearly invincible, amassing a treble, which included all major trophies, and four sparkling Premier League titles. Beckham's clever free-kick technique and impressive long-range goals were integral to his game, but his manufactured Hollywood image also played a significant role in his superstar status. Beckham became a global figure off the pitch through his marriage to Spice Girl Victoria Adams and the brand-building of his own trademark. Beckham maintained top professionalism during his 12-year tenure at Old Trafford, consistently delivering outstanding performances for the club.

Real Madrid and LA Galaxy

After leaving Manchester United, Beckham joined Real Madrid alongside Plymouth-based colleague Steve McManaman. He was presented as the club's latest 'galáctico', a set of world-famous players assembled between 2003 and 2009 as part of Florentino Pérez's famed sporting project 'Zidanes y Pavones'. Beckham's time in Spain brought renewed success on the pitch, delivering the La Liga title to Santiago Bernabéu in his fourth and final season with the club. Despite a few genuinely memorable moments in terms of silverware, Beckham's time in Spain increased his appeal in emerging football markets in the Far East and Asia, associating him with the widely recognizable white of Real Madrid.

Beckham's move to the west coast of the USA was a significant milestone in his career, benefiting both club and player. The announcement of Beckham's arrival at LA Galaxy was unique, especially since his then-current team manager, Fabio Capello, did not want the England captain to leave Spain. Beckham signed with the side based at The Home Depot Center in Carson, California. He made his debut for LA Galaxy in a pre-season friendly match against English Premier League side Chelsea when he was substituted in the 78th minute. Beckham's commitment to the project led to attendance records being set at LA Galaxy, with sell-out crowds eager to see the former England captain in action under the dazzling Major League Soccer (MLS) sun.

Beckham's move to MLS served to boost the popularity of 'Football' in the United States, away from the traditional version of the sport, American Football, which remains the country's most popular sport. His presence in MLS brought international attention to the league, inspiring a new generation of soccer fans and players. Beckham's impact on the sport in the United States extended beyond his playing career, as he remains a co-owner of LA Galaxy following his retirement.

Paris Saint-Germain and Beyond

Beckham's career continued to evolve, taking him to Paris Saint-Germain (PSG) in 2013. Joining PSG at the age of 37, Beckham's experience and leadership were invaluable to the team. He signed a five-month contract with PSG, and during his short stint, he helped the club secure the Ligue 1 title. Beckham's decision to donate his entire salary to a children's charity in Paris further enhanced his reputation as a compassionate and socially responsible athlete.

International Career

Beckham's contributions to the England national team were equally significant. He earned his first cap for England in 1996 and went on to make 115 appearances, scoring 17 goals. Beckham captained the national team for six years, leading England in three FIFA World Cups (1998, 2002, and 2006) and two UEFA European Championships (2000 and 2004). His leadership, precision, and ability to perform under pressure made him a key figure in England's national team history.

Critical Analysis and Legacy

Beckham's professional career was marked by his ability to adapt to different teams and cultures while maintaining a high level of performance. His versatility and consistency earned him respect and admiration from fans, teammates, and managers alike. Beckham's influence extended beyond the pitch, as he became a global brand ambassador for football and a role model for aspiring athletes.

In conclusion, David Beckham's professional football career is a testament to his skill, dedication, and versatility. From his early days at Manchester United to his global impact at Real Madrid, LA Galaxy, and PSG, Beckham's journey is a remarkable example of how an athlete can transcend the sport to become a global icon. His legacy as a footballer and cultural figure continues to inspire and shape the world of football.

Chapter 3: Beckham Off the Field

This chapter takes a closer look at David Beckham's influence beyond the pitch. The football icon is known as much for his style, fashion sense, and image as for his mastery with a football at his feet. He is a style icon and a trendsetter, with his iconic hairstyles and tattoos spawning copycat behavior from fans in the UK and around the world.

Fashion and Style Influence

As much as Beckham focused on his athletic endeavors, he has always been about fashion and style too. Starting back when he could only afford Adidas joggers, his interest in menswear has always been sincere, and his ability to wear clothes well intrigued fans and the media. When he became the face of leading brands like Emporio Armani, it was a natural, lucrative step. His rising status led to collections with Adidas, Belstaff, Kent & Curwen, and a grooming line he operates with the former CEO of L'Oréal. Kim Jones, the Artistic Director of menswear at Dior, has often turned to Beckham, not just for his image, but for more substantive input; there is a luxury touch to Beckham's sense of style.

Expanding on Beckham's Off-the-Field Influence

David Beckham's influence off the field is multifaceted, encompassing fashion, endorsements, philanthropy, and cultural impact. This chapter delves into the various aspects of Beckham's life beyond football, exploring how his off-the-pitch marketability has made him one of the most recognizable superstars on the planet.

Endorsements and Business Ventures

Beckham's marketability is unparalleled, and he has leveraged his fame to secure numerous endorsement deals with global brands. His partnerships with companies such as Adidas, Pepsi, H&M, and Armani have significantly boosted his income and global presence. Beckham's business acumen is evident in his ability to maintain long-term relationships with these brands, often becoming a central figure in their marketing campaigns. His collaborations go beyond mere endorsements; they often involve creative input, reflecting his personal style and influence.

Fashion and Style Influence (Continued)

Beckham's fashion journey began modestly, but his impact on the industry has been profound. As he gained fame, his sartorial choices became a focal point for media and fans alike. Beckham's style evolution from a sportswear enthusiast to a fashion icon has been marked by his ability to seamlessly blend classic and contemporary elements. His early fashion statements included bold hairstyles and distinctive outfits that set trends and inspired fans worldwide.

In 2005, Beckham's fashion influence began to take on a more refined and sophisticated tone. He embraced a more "shared" look that incorporated elements of Italian, French, and American menswear. His approach to fashion emphasized effortless simplicity, often rooted in a classic wardrobe but with modern twists. Stripes, checks, bold colors, and mixed materials became staples of his style, creating a high-low sensibility that resonated with a broad audience.

Beckham's fashion influence extended beyond personal style to significant collaborations with top designers and brands. His work with Emporio Armani, which featured iconic underwear campaigns, solidified his status as a global fashion icon. Subsequent collaborations with brands like Belstaff and Kent & Curwen showcased his versatility and commitment to quality. Beckham's grooming line, developed in partnership with the former CEO of L'Oréal, further cemented his influence in the fashion and beauty industries.

Kim Jones, Artistic Director of menswear at Dior, has often sought Beckham's input for his fashion expertise. Beckham's ability to navigate different fashion realms and contribute meaningfully to design processes highlights his deep understanding of the industry. His personal style, characterized by a luxury touch, has consistently set trends and influenced fashion narratives.

Cultural and Philanthropic Impact

Beckham's influence extends beyond fashion and endorsements to significant philanthropic efforts. He has been involved in numerous charitable activities, leveraging his fame and resources to support causes such as children's education, health, and disaster relief. Beckham's commitment to philanthropy has earned him respect and admiration, further enhancing his public image.

One notable example of Beckham's philanthropy is his work with UNICEF. As a UNICEF Goodwill Ambassador, he has actively participated in campaigns and initiatives aimed at improving the lives of children worldwide. His dedication to humanitarian causes demonstrates his desire to use his platform for positive change.

The Brand Beckham

The "Brand Beckham" phenomenon is a testament to the meticulous planning and strategic efforts behind David Beckham's universal appeal. A team of professionals, including managers, publicists, and marketing experts, has worked tirelessly to craft and maintain his image. This strategic approach has ensured that Beckham remains relevant and influential across different sectors.

David Roach, a sports professional and author, has extensively studied Beckham's off-the-field activities. Roach's work highlights how athletes can capitalize on their stardom through licensing and merchandising deals. Other journalists and authors have explored the reasons behind Beckham's enduring appeal, often attributing it to a combination of natural charisma, strategic branding, and a supportive team.

Influence on Personal Style and Pop Culture

Beckham's impact on personal style is evident in the way people around the world emulate his looks. His hairstyles, from the early "curtain" haircut to the later slicked-back styles, have inspired countless fans. Tattoos, another signature aspect of Beckham's look, have become a significant part of his identity and have influenced tattoo culture globally.

Beckham's influence extends to various aspects of pop culture. His appearances in advertisements, magazines, and television shows have made him a household name. His marriage to Victoria Beckham, a former Spice Girl and successful fashion designer, has further amplified his celebrity status, making the couple a power duo in the worlds of sports and fashion.

Conclusion

David Beckham's influence beyond the pitch is as significant as his accomplishments on it. His ability to seamlessly transition from footballer to fashion icon, business mogul, and philanthropist is a testament to his versatility and charisma. Beckham's enduring appeal and impact on various industries make him a unique and influential figure in contemporary culture.

Chapter 4: Beckham's Impact on Pop Culture

The August 2007 article estimated Beckham's 2006 earnings at $33 million. This context highlights his significant presence in pop culture as a pitchman and entertainer. This final chapter delves into Beckham's brand endorsements and collaborations, examining the important intersections of sports, entertainment, and consumer culture. It explores how "Brand Beckham" parallels other iconic brands, such as Air Jordan, and solidifies Beckham's place in popular culture from the late 1990s to 2010.

The previous chapters have demonstrated that David Beckham is fundamentally a footballer. However, his multifarious cultural involvements—as a model, designer, author, advertising pitchman, actor, performer, and social figure—cement his status within popular culture. The narrative between Beckham as an advertiser and consumer culture reveals shared fantasies of eternal, seductive promise that Beckham gracefully, if sometimes unwittingly, embodies. His enduring relationship with Adidas and other brands underscores his powerful position earned through years of commitment and success.

Celebrity Endorsements and Brand Collaborations

David Beckham is not only a talented football athlete who excels on the pitch but also an international style icon that transcends gender and ethnicity. Football and entertainment often interact and influence each other, producing a complex social and cultural output. Football fans' orientation towards their clubs can influence their orientation towards their celebrity fans. Celebrity advocates resonate with fans and develop different status symbols than traditional consumers by forming personal bonds with their audience. These lessons and experiences have helped transform Beckham into a billionaire brand.

Early Endorsements

Beckham's engagement with culture, fashion, and style has also been channeled through various celebrity endorsements. His first significant endorsement came in 1997 with Brylcreem. This partnership marked the beginning of a series of high-profile endorsements, from pharmaceutical products and sports drinks to fashion brands and perfume lines. Beckham's early endorsements showcased his versatility and appeal beyond the football pitch.

High-Profile Brand Collaborations

Over the years, Beckham has established himself as a leading figure in the world of endorsements. His collaborations with brands like Adidas, Pepsi, H&M, and Armani have significantly boosted his global presence and income. These partnerships are not just commercial ventures; they reflect Beckham's personal style and influence. For instance, his iconic underwear campaigns for Armani helped solidify his status as a fashion icon and expanded his reach into the fashion industry.

The Beckham Brand

Beckham's image is a carefully crafted blend of athleticism, style, and charisma. His range of aftershaves and colognes, as well as the numerous magazines featuring his personal range of products, highlight his ability to market himself effectively. Brand collaborations, such as those with Adidas and H&M, have helped cement Beckham's image as a footballing, family, style, and fashion icon. These collaborations emphasize high-quality production, sophisticated design, and direct involvement from Beckham, including naming rights and philanthropic support from UNICEF, further enhancing his personal relationships with his audience.

The Power of Endorsements

Beckham's endorsements have extended beyond traditional advertising. He has designed American football endorsement lines, and collaborated on limited edition shoes with designers like Paul Smith. His influence even reached the music industry, with groups like Sugababes recording songs for Karl Lagerfeld and Girls Aloud endorsing L'Oréal. These partnerships showcase Beckham's ability to transcend different industries and appeal to a wide audience.

Strategic Brand Management

David Roach's extensive study on Beckham's off-the-field activities highlights how athletes can capitalize on their stardom through licensing and merchandising deals. Other journalists and authors have explored the reasons behind Beckham's enduring appeal, often attributing it to a combination of natural charisma, strategic branding, and a supportive team. The "Brand Beckham" phenomenon is a testament to meticulous planning and strategic efforts, ensuring Beckham remains relevant and influential across different sectors.

Cultural and Philanthropic Impact

Beckham's influence extends beyond endorsements to significant philanthropic efforts. His work with UNICEF and various charitable activities demonstrate his commitment to using his platform for positive change. Beckham's philanthropy has earned him respect and admiration, further enhancing his public image. For example, as a UNICEF Goodwill Ambassador, he has actively participated in campaigns and initiatives aimed at improving the lives of children worldwide. His dedication to humanitarian causes showcases his desire to leverage his fame for social good.

Conclusion

David Beckham's impact on pop culture is as significant as his accomplishments on the football pitch. His seamless transition from athlete to style icon, business mogul, and philanthropist underscores his versatility and charisma. Beckham's brand endorsements and collaborations highlight the intersections of sports, entertainment, and consumer culture, demonstrating his unique ability to captivate and influence a global audience. His enduring appeal and contributions to various industries make him a quintessential figure in contemporary culture.

Chapter 5: Beckham's Philanthropic Work

David Beckham's contributions off the field extend far beyond his roles in fashion and entertainment; he is also deeply committed to philanthropic work. This chapter explores Beckham's significant impact through various charitable endeavors, particularly highlighting his role as a UNICEF Goodwill Ambassador and his other philanthropic initiatives.

UNICEF Ambassadorship

David Beckham became a UNICEF Goodwill Ambassador in 2005, leveraging his global fame to advocate for children's rights worldwide. UNICEF selects public figures with a strong commitment and proven ability to communicate effectively about children's issues. Beckham's dedication to social responsibility, through both his foundation and other projects, made him an ideal representative for the organization.

Throughout his tenure as a UNICEF Ambassador, Beckham has consistently participated in projects aimed at improving children's lives. One notable example was his appearance at the launch of Unite Against AIDS in India and at the 2003 State of the World's Children launch in Delhi. Despite earning a significantly lower salary compared to his football career, Beckham remained devoted to his philanthropic efforts. He carried the Olympic flame on April 6, 2012, in Athens, participated in a special Handover Ceremony in London the following day, and attended a UNICEF-supported children's event in Manchester on July 23, 2012.

The Seven Fund

Beckham is one of the founders of the Seven Fund, a charitable project run by the Howgreat Brands Company. The fund involves a $1 million donation from individuals worldwide, invested in seven social-impact initiatives. These initiatives aim to tackle poverty by improving issues related to water, air, waste, and consumerism, with returns expected within 12 months. The fund also seeks to continue Beckham's legacy in the fashion industry, addressing the current negative attitudes towards fashion's association with carbon emissions.

Broader Philanthropic Efforts

Beckham's philanthropic impact extends beyond his work with UNICEF. His career and global influence have allowed him to support various causes across different countries, ages, and interests. Literature often suggests that fans use celebrity associations with products in consumer culture, valuing brands perceived as important through their connection with celebrities. Instructional manipulations influenced self- and other evaluations, suggesting that celebrity attachment has a moderate and variable influence on outcomes, as consumers establish initial relationships with celebrities.

Further Contributions and Influence

In the book 'David Beckham: Twenty Years in the Making,' Beckham reflects on his decorated football career, accompanied by photographs by Dean Freeman. A limited edition of the book, signed by Beckham, was distributed to a select range of people. Beckham's influence extends beyond football and books; he is a significant charitable figure. In 2015, he ranked 61st on Forbes' list of The World's

Highest-Paid Athletes, earning $65 million, which he claimed to do for charity. His Instagram bio subtly emphasizes his commitment to charitable work, stating: "I AM IN THIS RICH, I AM IN THIS CHAIR, AND I AM IN THIS SIGNATURE - DAVID BECK-HAM."

Beckham's dedication to charity work is evident in various initiatives. For example, he participated in Globe Tattoo Day with UNICEF and other organizations, aiming to combat typhoons. His role as an ambassador for UNICEF in 2005 marked the beginning of a long-standing commitment to educating and mobilizing the world through online platforms and in-person presentations, when possible. In 2015, he collaborated on the Unite Against Ebola project, visiting orphans at the Ebola Treatment Centre in Sierra Leone. Beckham's efforts raised over £3 million for UNICEF in 2016.

Conclusion

David Beckham's philanthropic work is a testament to his dedication to making a positive impact on the world. His role as a UNICEF Goodwill Ambassador, founding of the Seven Fund, and various charitable initiatives highlight his commitment to social responsibility and helping those in need. Beckham's philanthropic legacy continues to inspire and mobilize efforts to improve the lives of children and communities worldwide.

Conclusion

The aura surrounding David Beckham transcends age, nationality, and fan following, making it both straightforward and complex to assess his impact. As a footballer, Beckham commanded a polarizing presence, attracting both ardent supporters and extreme critics. His tenure as England's captain, where he became one of the few players to surpass 100 international caps, highlights his exceptional contributions to the sport. Beckham's personal accolades can be divided into two parts: his technical prowess and his persona. His distinctive appearance, characterized by his yellow-bleached hair, red-and-white wristbands, and Under Armour gear, embodied a never-say-die attitude, reminiscent of a Hollywood hero. Beyond his athleticism, Beckham epitomized discipline, hard work, and wisdom from experience.

Known as 'Goldenballs,' Beckham's good looks and fashion sense cemented his status as a style icon. He is often hailed as the epitome of a stylish gentleman, blending influences from gangster and punk styles. Ockham's razor would refute any attempt to undermine either of his careers—football or fashion—as he excelled at the highest levels in both. Beckham's life seamlessly moved between the parallel universes of sports and style, showcasing his versatility and ability to captivate audiences worldwide.

The Victorians coined the phrase "clothes make the man," and David Beckham exemplifies this adage. Whether on the field as 'legendary Becks' or in front of the cameras as 'goldenheart,' Beckham's influence extends far beyond the turf. His legacy encompasses facets of his influence as a footballer, style icon, and cultural phenomenon, endorsing the belief that 'somebody is up there acting as a performer to perfection.'

Summary of Key Findings

The primary objective of this essay was to explore David Beckham's impact on football and fashion in the 21st century. By examining the trajectory of Beckham's career, we aimed to present his legacy and how he managed to remain a household name long after retiring from professional football. Beckham evolved from a national hero to an international celebrity, adopting a new identity in the 2000s. He transitioned from being solely a footballer to becoming an advertising figure with a stylish presence, playing for Real Madrid and LA Galaxy and appearing alongside celebrities like Angelina Jolie.

As a 20th-century legend, Beckham embraced a new role through philanthropic work and mentorship. By discussing Beckham's influence on 21st-century football and fashion, we were able to tell his story from the perspective of a fan, fashion lover, and individual directly affected by his phenomenon. Beckham's versatility as a sportsman and his sense of style have touched countless lives, making him more than just a footballer. He became a trendsetter and role model, rising to fame not only for his football skills but also for his off-pitch persona and profound impact on the fashion industry.

Beckham has become a cultural symbol of fashion, characterized by his many hairstyles, tattoos, clothing lines, and charity work. He is often regarded as one of the most attractive footballers in the world, with a significantly higher level of appeal than other well-known players. This study evaluated Beckham's style to understand how he evolved from a footballer into a fashion figure within the media landscape, sports industry, sociology, enterprise, and marketing. The essay discussed Beckham's role in the development of style in the games and various facets of lifestyle, branding, and administration.

The impact of style on modern trends and society is significant, and Beckham's influence in this regard is profound. His ability to enhance societal understanding of large themes and meanings underscores his position as a cultural icon. Having been in a position of power and wealth, Beckham embraced a wider duty to encourage societal adjustments. The Beckham heritage clarifies his broader social perceptions and moral norms, continuing to affect us today.

Final Thoughts

David Beckham's legacy is multifaceted, encompassing his achievements as a footballer, style icon, philanthropist, and cultural phenomenon. His ability to captivate audiences on and off the field, inspire societal change, and set trends in fashion and lifestyle makes him a unique and influential figure in contemporary culture. Beckham's journey from the pitch to global icon serves as a testament to his versatility, charisma, and enduring impact on the world.

References

Adams, Tim. N.d. "David Beckham and the Art of Managing a Global Sport Brand." *The Observer.*

Bennett, Oliver. 2017. "In the Frame: The Rise of David Beckham's Eyewear Range." *Financial Times.*

Best, Jamie. 2020. "A History of David Beckham's Headwear." *GQ.*

Blasik, Joanna. 2020. "Introducing Deyvid: Socio-Cultural Aspects of the Americanisation of David Beckham's Identity." *Journal of Sport and Social Issues.*

Carrington, Simon. N.d. "Explained: The Science of David Beckham's Free-Kicks and How He Revolutionised Football." *The Conversation.*

Caulton, Teresa. N.d. "How David Beckham Changed the Face of Celebrity Fragrance Forever." *Grazia.*

Crane, Simon. 2013. "How David Beckham Invented Modern Menswear." *Highsnobiety.*

Cronin, Mike. 2014. "Marmite Sport TV Stars: David Beckham and Roy Keane a Case Study in Differences." *Television New Media* 15 (3): 238-250. doi:10.1177/1527476412471926.

García-Manso, Aurora, and Alberto Núñez-Pomar. 2013. "Pasión y dolor se unen en sus reflejos." *El País.*

Hornbuckle, Myles. 2018. "Watch What Happens When an Englishman Teaches David Beckham How to Make a Cup of Tea." *Forbes.*

Jackson, David. N.d. "David Beckham: Soccer Star and Coveted Model?" *Financial Times.*

"London's Most Influential Los Angeles Natives, from Tahar Rahim to Romeo Beckham: Meet the Future of the Industry." *Dazed*.

Long, David. 2018. "David Beckham: Icon for an Island Story." *International Journal of the Arts in Societies* 12 (3): 9-34.

Olajubu, Omolola Be'Ebeyinchini. 2012. "From David to Victoria: The Branding of the Beckhams." *ESP: Journal of English for Academic Purposes*, 1(1), 31-49.

Olajubu, Omolola, and Dzwairo Charity. 2013. "The Power of the Beckham Brand: Celebrity Influence in Sports Products Marketing Strategies." *International Journal of Business Management and Economic Research (IJBMER)*, 4(3), 303-321.

O'Rorke, Evelyn. 2018. "The David Beckham Effect." *MR PORTER*.

Pope, Phoebe. 2019. "David Beckham's Game-Changing Grooming Blur that Banishes Wine." *Vogue*.

Copyright Disclaimer

9 798348 108366